How Things Grow

From Tadpole to Frog

By Jan Kottke

Welcome Books

Children's Press
A Division of Grolier Publishing
New York / London / Hong Kong / Sydney
Danbury, Connecticut

Photo Credits: Cover and all photos © Dwight Kuhn

Contributing Editors: Mark Beyer and Eliza Berkowitz
Book Design: MaryJane Wojciechowski

Visit Children's Press on the Internet at:
http://publishing.grolier.com

Library of Congress Cataloging-in-Publication Data

Kottke, Jan.
    From tadpole to frog / by Jan Kottke.
      p. cm. — (How things grow)
    Includes bibliographical references and index.
    Summary: Simple text and photographs explain how a tadpole becomes a frog.
    ISBN 0-516-23311-4 (lib. bdg.) — ISBN 0-516-23511-7 (pbk.)
    1. Frogs—Life cycles—Juvenile literature. 2. Tadpoles—Juvenile literature.
      [1. Frogs. 2. Tadpoles.] I. Title.
QL668.E2 K68 2000
  597.8'9139—dc21   00-024376

Contents

A frog **egg** is laid in a **pond**.

The black dot is a **growing** frog.

It is very small.

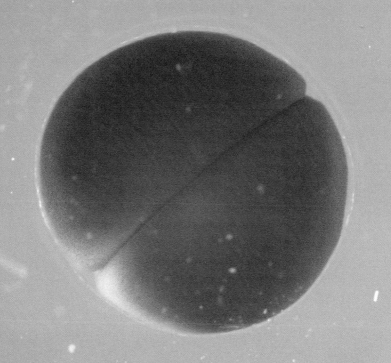

5

The black dot becomes a **tadpole**.

Its tail is growing.

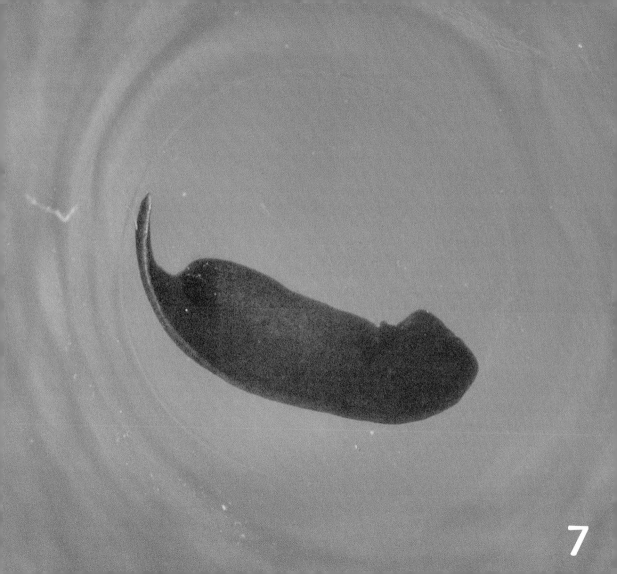
7

The tadpole has **hatched** from its egg.

It has a long tail and a small mouth.

9

Legs grow from the tadpole's body.

The back legs grow longer than the front legs.

The tadpole is becoming a frog.

Its tail becomes shorter.

Its eyes and mouth grow larger.

The frog climbs out of the pond.

It is still growing.

15

The frog is now grown-up.

Its tail is gone.

17

The grown-up frog doesn't look like a tadpole anymore.

It can now climb out of the water when it wants to.

A frog makes noises so that other frogs can hear it.

Ribbit.

Ribbit.

21

New Words

egg (**ehg**) round object that holds a growing animal

growing (**groh**-ing) getting bigger

hatched (**hacht**) came out of an egg

pond (**pond**) a small body of water

tadpole (**tad**-pohl) a baby frog

To Find Out More

Books
From Tadpole to Frog
by Gerald Legg
Franklin Watts

Tale of a Tadpole
by Barbara Ann Porte
Orchard Books

Web Sites
Frogland!
http://allaboutfrogs.org
This site has a lot of fun frog things to do. There is a frog coloring book, an art gallery, and many links to other frog sites.

Frogs!
http://www.seagrant.wisc.edu/madisonjason10/frogs.html
Check out this site to learn more about frogs. You can listen to frog noises, take a frog quiz, and read an interview with a scientist.

Index

About the Author
Jan Kottke is the owner/director of several preschools in the Tidewater area of Virginia. A lifelong early education professional, she is completing a phonics reading series for preschoolers.

Reading Consultants
Kris Flynn, Coordinator, Small School District Literacy, The San Diego County Office of Education

Shelly Forys, Certified Reading Recovery Specialist, W.J. Zahnow Elementary School, Waterloo, IL

Peggy McNamara, Professor, Bank Street College of Education, Reading and Literacy Program